Tons
of Trash

Tons of Trash

Why You Should Recycle and What Happens When You Do

JOAN RATTNER HEILMAN

Illustrated by Nancy Schill

AN AVON CAMELOT BOOK

TONS OF TRASH is an original publication of Avon Books. This work has never before appeared in book form.

AVON BOOKS
A division of
The Hearst Corporation
1350 Avenue of the Americas
New York, New York 10019

Contents

Tons of Trash

1

Let's Go on a Trip

Have you ever wondered what happens to the old newspapers you save for recycling? Do you know the mysterious journey a used detergent bottle takes after it leaves the recycling center before it's turned into other things, such as a carpet, a shoulder pad, or a park bench? Maybe you'd like to go along with a bale of tin cans while it gets ready to become part of a new car, a steel beam, or more cans. Or perhaps you want to accompany a glass jar to a recycling plant where it prepares for its new life as a soda bottle or a piece of pavement on the street.

We're going to take you on a trip to find out what happens to all those things you used to throw in the garbage but now you save for recycling.

1

Where do they go? What is done with them? What will they be when we meet them again?

First we'll tour a primary processing center, called a MRF (pronounced MURF) or materials recovery facility. Here the recyclables are sorted and sometimes shredded or baled, ready to be shipped out in big tractor-trailer trucks to the mills that will make new products out of their raw materials. Then we will move on to the mills or recycling plants to find out what happens next.

A Rundown on Recycling

Recycling means making something new and useful out of something we don't want anymore. When we use old things to make new things instead of throwing them into the garbage can, we are recycling because we are using the same raw materials over and over again. And that's good because it helps the environment.

Not everything can be recycled, and some things are harder to use again than others. But a lot of our leftovers can be used again—and again—and again. Glass, for example, is 100 percent recyclable and can be reused forever. The same is true of steel and other metals. Paper can go around four or five times, and some kinds of plastic have at least a couple of lives in their future.

In fact, experts think that, if we put our minds to it, we could find a new use for almost all of our trash. Just think of how many things you can already recycle instead of throwing them away, such as cat-food cans, jelly jars, cardboard boxes, wire hangers, shampoo bottles, even broken washing machines and worn-out cars.

Why Bother?

Recycling or making new things out of old things saves our natural resources. By recycling old paper, we create new paper without cutting down more trees. When we reuse old cans or bottles, we reduce the need to mine and drill the land for ores and other materials. Plastic comes from crude oil and natural gas, so using it again slows down the consumption of these limited resources.

Recycling saves a lot of energy. Using the same materials over again requires far less energy than making something with ingredients that are new. And that results in another advantage—less pollution.

Recycling saves money. It is cheaper because it reduces the amount of trash going into the waste stream so your town doesn't have to pay to bury or burn it. Getting rid of our garbage is very expensive. And, finally, it helps to save the Earth, because we are running out of space to dump it.

So, do your part to save the world from being buried in garbage! Get your whole family—and everybody else you know—to recycle. If your town doesn't already have a good recycling program, put the pressure on your local officials to start one now. You'll help write a happy ending to a trashy story!

Where Does All the Garbage Come From?

It comes from *us*. We all throw out an awful lot of stuff. We like to use something once and toss it—like paper towels, plastic knives and forks, bottles, paper cups, lunch bags, even cameras, razors, and pens. We like to buy things in fancy wrappings that look good but go straight into the trash can. And we don't like old things very much even if they are still good. So we throw them away and buy new ones, all sorts of things like socks and pants and bikes and toys.

In fact, the average American produces about four pounds of garbage every single day, which adds up to enough to fill a line of 10-ton garbage trucks stretched halfway to the moon. In a year, each of us, on average, has thrown away almost three-quarters of a ton of trash!

Down in the Dumps

Nobody knows what to do with all of our trash anymore. For centuries in America, we dumped our leftovers over the side of the nearest hill or down a pit or into a swamp. Or we fed them to the pigs. Did you know that 100 hungry pigs can eat a ton of garbage a day?

Then, as cities and towns grew, we began burying our trash in landfills, empty land on the edge of town, and covering it over with layers of dirt or plastic. We thought it would biodegrade (break down through the action of bacteria and fungi) or photodegrade (break down by exposure to light) and go away. We started towing it out to sea on barges and dumping it into the ocean, but even the oceans can't handle all that pollution. And finally we started building incinerators where we could toss anything we didn't want anymore and burn it up in huge furnaces.

But now almost all of the landfills in this country are full and nobody wants new ones in their neighborhood. Many of them, too, have been closed down because a lot of what we throw away contains toxic chemicals. Over the years, these dangerous substances leak into the ground with the rainwater, contaminating the soil, the air we breathe, and the aquifers that provide our drinking water.

Some materials—such as plastic and aluminum—will never, never degrade. And other garbage—like food, paper, wood, iron, and cloth—needs air and sunlight to break down. In a tightly packed landfill, it gets so little air and sunlight that it doesn't change very much for decades or even centuries. Scientists have dug up 30-year-old hot dogs that still looked almost the same as the day they were buried, carrots that were still orange, and newspapers that you could still read.

Up in Smoke

So why not burn all our trash up? The answer is, we can't possibly build enough incinerators to handle all the garbage we make. Besides, burning garbage in incinerators pollutes the air with poisonous gases and produces toxic residues that must be buried somewhere. But where? Not in my backyard!

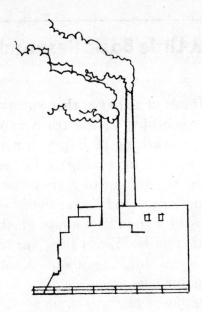

Trash Prevention

One way to deal with garbage is to stop making so much of it. Don't buy too many throwaway things like paper cups and plastic forks that come with a one-way ticket to the dump. Find good ways to use other things over again. And recycle everything you possibly can.

Recycling is an important part of the solution to today's problem of what to do with all our garbage. You may already have a recycling program where you live. If not, your community will surely start one soon. It's the law in many states, and besides, it's the smart thing to do.

A Little Basic Research

Today most of us have "throwaway" habits. Tossing something in the trash can is a lot easier than washing it, fixing it, using it for something else, or saving it for recycling. That's why the volume of garbage we produce is growing larger and larger every year.

Just to get a good idea about all the things a typical family like yours throws away without even thinking about it, check out your own garbage cans.

After a day of heavy use, maybe after a party or a family dinner, go through the contents of the cans and make a list of every single thing you find. It's a messy job, so you may want to wear rubber gloves. But think of it this way: only a few hours ago, most of this trash was on your plate, in the frying pan, in your room, or in your closet.

List all your garbage in the following categories:

1. Paper
2. Food waste
3. Plastic
4. Glass
5. Metal
6. Other (everything that doesn't fit into the other groups, such as wood, yard waste, rubber, cloth)

Now, decide how much of this stuff is recyclable or reusable. Unless you live in a family that already takes recycling seriously, you'll be amazed at the amount that can be saved.

Note: Remember that food scraps (except for meat and fish products) can be recycled too. If you have a yard, add them to the compost pile or dig a hole in the garden and cover them with dirt. In only a couple of weeks, they will biodegrade into rich new soil!

Glossary

Aquifer: An underground layer of water.

Biodegrade: To break down or decompose by the action of living organisms (bacteria or fungi).

Incinerators: Furnaces that burn up trash.

Ingredients: The individual parts of a mixture.

MRF: A materials recovery facility where recyclables are sorted and separated.

Photodegrade: To break down or decompose by the action of certain kinds of light such as sunlight.

Raw materials: Materials in their natural or original state.

Recyclables: Things that can now be collected, separated, processed, and made into new products.

Residues: Leftovers.

Toxic: Poisonous

Waste stream: All the wastes of a community.

2

Treasures in the Trash

Once you've got the hang of it, it's easy for you and your family to save things for recycling instead of throwing them in the garbage can. But, after you save them and your town collects them from the curb in front of your house or at a drop-off center, that's not the end of it. There's lots more work to be done to get them ready to be made into something else.

First of all, the recyclables must be separated because each kind of material will be sold to a different buyer. After all, a glass manufacturer has no use for paper, metal, or plastics. And a plastics processing plant has no interest whatsoever in glass, paper, or metal.

What's more, most plastics processing plants

want only certain kinds of plastics—and they want them clean. Metal recyclers are very fussy about what metals they will accept. Some glass makers will take bottles of only one color and most will turn down loads of mixed colors. Paper mills may reject loads of newspapers that contain too many magazines, telephone books, or pieces of junk mail.

Let the MRF Do It

In many towns and cities today, the recyclables are trucked off, all mixed up together except for paper and big metal appliances, to a MRF (materials recovery facility). The MRF is a transfer station which sorts them all out and packages them neatly, just the way the mills want them.

Recyclable materials don't always go to MRFs. Sometimes they are sent directly from your town to brokers who sell them to companies in the United States or foreign countries. And sometimes they go straight to scrap processors who deal with one kind of material. But, for more and more communities, the MRF is the way to go because it's easier to send everything to one place.

What Goes On at a MRF?

The MRF is a very busy, noisy, smelly, messy place where machines and people with hard hats and strong backs work hard all day long. Their job is to make order out of chaos, sifting and sorting the mountains of trash that arrive by the truckload hour after hour, decontaminating them, compressing them into bales, or grinding them up and sorting them in bins.

Every MRF is different and each one of them uses its own methods of getting all the recyclables ready to be sent to their end users. Some are quite simple while others are "state of the art," modern and automated. But here's what happens every day at a typical MRF:

The garbage trucks or big tractor-trailers that rumble over the highways from your town to the nearest MRF dump their loads in big piles onto a "tipping floor" inside an open shed or into a "receiving pit."

If the load is a truckful of newspapers, workers loosen up the papers and pick out most of the contaminants, such as magazines and telephone books. Then they use forklifts to push the papers onto a conveyor that moves them to an automatic baler. The baler compresses them into huge blocks and ties them up with wire or plastic strapping. Now the newspapers are ready for shipping to a paper mill.

Picky Picky

Sometimes trucks pull up to the MRF with loads of glass or plastic or metals that have already been

13

separated at a town recycling center. But, in most cases, the loads contain these materials all mixed up together (comingled). Then a lot of work must be done to separate them.

After a comingled load is dumped out into giant multicolored mounds, bulldozers push the piles onto moving conveyor belts where they pass through magnets and blowers. Now the different materials part ways. The steel cans are picked out by the powerful magnets and sent down a special chute. The blowers, called air classifiers, blast the lighter materials—aluminum cans and plastics— up into the air and off into their own containers.

The glass bottles and jars, left behind, drop onto another conveyor where the quick hands of many workers separate them by color—clear, green, and brown. At most MRFs, they are then fed into a grinder that crushes them into tiny pieces called cullet. The cullet is stored in big bins until it is sent to a glass manufacturing plant. Sometimes, however, whole uncrushed bottles are shipped out and the grinding is done at the plant.

The steel cans, meanwhile, are crushed and compacted into 3,500-pound bales.

But the plastics haven't finished their trip yet. They need still another sorting before they're ready to leave the MRF for the mill. First washed with heated water under high compression, they

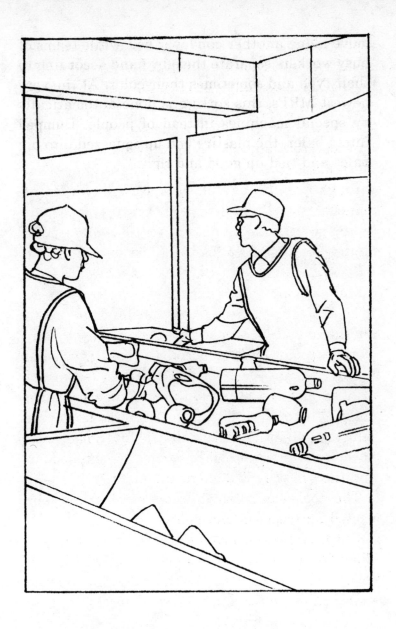

move along another conveyor belt while teams of busy workers separate them by hand according to their type and sometimes their color. At the very newest MRFs, this sorting is done automatically by special machines instead of people. Dumped into a baler, the plastics end up squeezed into big bales and tied up good and tight.

Glossary

Broker: Person or agency that buys and sells things.

Comingled: Mixed together.

Compress: Press together.

Compression: Pressure.

Contaminants: Harmful or unwanted substances.

Conveyor: A continuous mechanical belt that carries things from one place to another.

Cullet: Crushed glass.

Decontaminate: Remove harmful or unwanted substances.

End user: The manufacturer or processor that produces the final product.

Forklift: A device, usually mounted on a truck, with strong prongs that lift things.

Multicolored: Of many colors.

Receiving pit: A depression or hole where things are dumped.

Tipping floor: A floor on which things are dumped.

Transfer station: A place where things are collected and perhaps processed before being transferred to another place.

Things You Can Do at School

- Organize a recycling club at your school. Ask a teacher to help you and start a program for students and teachers to recycle newspapers, office paper, cans, glass, plastics, batteries, and anything else your town will accept. Work with your local officials to find out what to recycle, how to collect it, and what to do with it.

- Make posters and flyers reminding everyone what, where, and how to recycle. Make some to take home to your family and friends.

- Get your whole class to write to manufacturers, asking them to reduce the amounts of their unnecessary packaging. Ask them to use packing materials that can be recycled.

- Get your whole class, perhaps your whole school, to write letters to the national headquarters of fast-food restaurants that use non-recyclable materials and ask them to make changes. Tell them that, until they take some positive steps, you will not go to their restaurants.

18

- Pack your lunch in reusable containers, then take them home again for tomorrow. Use a lunch box so you won't need a bag. Take a thermos bottle instead of disposable drink containers.

- Ask your school principal to replace throwaway plates, glasses, and utensils in the cafeteria with durable ones that can be washed and used for a long time.

- Ask your teacher to take the class on a field trip to the supermarkets in your town. Talk to the store managers about stocking up on recycled and recyclable products. If necessary, get the class to write to the presidents of the stores, asking for changes that will help the environment.

- Don't throw recyclable things into the wastebasket. Deposit them in the appropriate bins at school or take them home for recycling. Remind your friends to do the same.

Things <u>You</u> Can Do at Home

- Start a recycling center at home. Decorate individual boxes or big brown paper bags and label them "returnables," "metals," "glass," "plastics," "newspapers," "batteries," and anything else that's recycled in your community. When they are full, take the recyclables to your drop-off center or put them at the curb on your appointed collection day.

- Use things over again, such as wrapping paper, ribbons, boxes, bags, lumber, fabric, string, buttons, yarn.

- Use grocery bags to line the garbage pail.

- Use both sides of the paper for notes. Use the backs of used sheets for scratch paper.

- Take old books and magazines to the library, nursing homes, hospitals, or exchange them with friends.

- Get your parents to take their used motor oil and car batteries to a service station for recycling.

- Wash out plastic bags, aluminum foil, food trays, pie pans, etc., and use them over again.

- Use plastic or glass containers for storing leftovers and packing your lunch.

- Don't throw anything out that's still useful. If you don't want it, give it away to someone who does.

- Remind your family not to throw reusable or recyclable things out. Encourage your family—and your friends—to recycle, and help them do it.

- Write to companies that send you catalogs, magazines, and newsletters that you don't want and ask them to take your name off their lists. You may also write to the Direct Marketing Association, 11 West 42nd Street, New York, NY 10163-3861, and ask them to remove your name from mailing lists.

- Buy the best-quality things you can afford, keep them in good condition, repair them if they break, and don't discard them simply because they aren't new anymore.

- Minimize your use of paper napkins and paper towels.

- If you have a garden, don't throw away your kitchen scraps (except for animal or fish products) or yard waste. Try composting them instead.

- Start a "swap box" for things that you don't want anymore but someone else might.

3

The Mysterious Journey of a Recycled Newspaper

Newspapers are made from ground-up trees—or from old newspapers. So, when you collect your papers for recycling, you are saving trees. It takes 25 to 40 years to grow a big tree and, to make sure of a steady supply, many paper manufacturers today plant their own forests with a new tree for every one they cut down.

Trees are good for us and for the environment. They are not only beautiful to look at, but they shade us from the sun, help clean the air we breathe, and fight global warming. They hold the soil so it doesn't wash away when it rains. They provide homes for thousands of species of birds and animals. When they die, they become new soil where more plants can grow.

Recycling newspapers not only saves trees but it helps the environment in other ways too. Making paper from old paper instead of new wood produces less air and water pollution, and doesn't require anywhere near as much energy.

Getting Your Newspapers Ready

1. Stack them.

2. Keep them dry.

3. Remove anything that isn't newspaper.

4. Tie the newspapers in bundles or leave them loose, depending on your program's requirements.

Plenty of Paper

Newspapers tell you what's going on in the world, but when you've finished reading them, they turn into garbage. So do all the other kinds of paper we use all day long from the moment we get up in the morning until we go to bed at night.

Americans throw away so much waste paper every day that it makes up about 40 percent of our municipal solid waste (fancy words for garbage). Newspapers alone account for about 8 percent by weight of all the trash in landfills. One ton of them takes up 3.3 cubic yards of space.

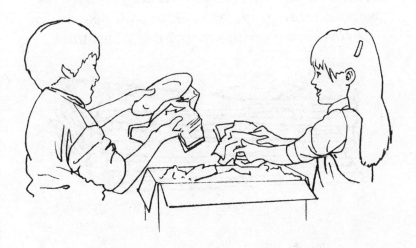

Sometimes old newspapers are handy around the house. You can line the cat's litter box with them, pack dishes in them when you're moving, or use them for mopping up messes. But you're still going to have plenty left over to save for recycling when you're done. Pile them up and keep them clean and dry. Don't include any other kinds of paper.

A lot of recycled newspapers become new newspapers, although some are turned into packing boxes, egg cartons, insulation, greeting cards, toilet paper, tissue paper, animal bedding, wallboard, paper towels, or other paper products.

When you save your newspapers after your family has read them, do you know what happens to them after that? Here's the trip they usually take before they're delivered back to your doorstep or the corner store with another day's headlines.

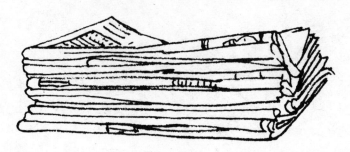

Where Does It Go?

Your old newspapers may be picked up at the curb in front of your house, thrown into trucks, and carted away. Or perhaps you take your piles of papers to your local recycling center. Either way, they soon get shipped off to a broker who sells them directly to an interested buyer or they are taken to a MRF for sorting and baling before going to a paper mill.

Arriving at the Paper Mill

Huge tractor-trailers rumble over the highways carrying full loads of old newspapers to the paper mill. Usually, the papers are squeezed into big cubes called bales and held together tightly with wire or strong strapping.

The trucks take the newspapers to the mill and dump them out. First, all the bales are opened and the papers loosened up. Then they are shoved onto a wide conveyor belt.

Turned into Pulp Slurry

The automatic conveyor feeds the paper into a big tub called a pulper. The pulper's job is to turn the paper back into wood pulp or fiber. It is a giant blender, an enormous vat with big paddle blades on the bottom, full of hot water and some strong chemical de-inkers whose purpose is to separate all the ink from the pulp.

After a few minutes of swirling around in the pulper, the old newspapers become a very sloppy mess called "slurry." The slurry looks like a big bowl of mushy gray oatmeal.

Now the pulp is pushed by centrifugal force through a series of screens with openings that become smaller and smaller. The screens remove unwanted materials or contaminants such as dirt, stones, paper clips, and staples.

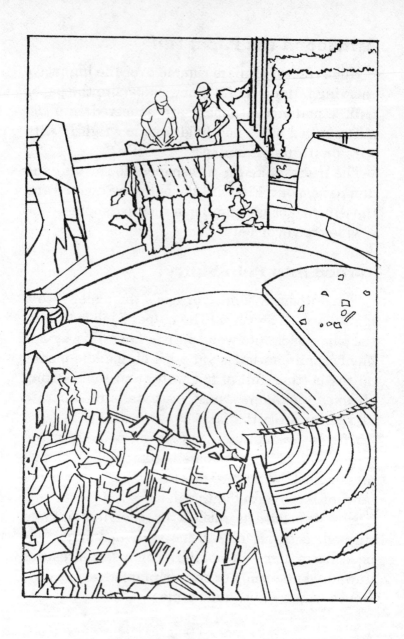

Time for a Bath

After all the junk is filtered out, the mixture of pulp and water is squeezed through several big rollers and flushed with clear water to rinse all the chemicals from the fiber. Or, in some mills, it may be run through rotating hollow cylinders with walls made of fine mesh. The water and any remaining impurities are swirled out through the mesh while the pulp remains behind.

The rinse cycle also washes out the very short wood fibers and leaves the longer, stronger ones that are required for new paper.

Hocus Pocus! Pulp Turns into Paper!

Now the pulp is doused with more water and starts its trip through a big paper-making machine called a fourdrinier. This machine can be as long as two or three football fields laid end to end. Its job is to change the watery mess back into paper.

At the beginning of its travels through the paper-making machine, the pulp is squirted over an endless wire screen that runs around and around on rollers. As the water drains out through the screen, the wood fibers—each one no more than a tenth of an inch long and as fine as your own hair—start sticking together. Soon the millions of tiny fibers bond tightly together to form a sheet.

When the sheet is strong enough, it moves on to the dryers. These are huge steam-heated rollers that iron the bonded fibers over and over again, gradually drying out all the water. Finally, the paper is wound up into huge rolls of newsprint that are cut by big sharp knives into smaller ones ready to be shipped off to a newspaper printing plant and a new life.

Now that's magic!

Glossary

Centrifugal force: The force that pulls things to the outside as they rotate rapidly around a center.

Cubic yard: An area that has the volume of one yard (three feet) in width, length, and depth.

Energy: Heat.

Global warming: The theory that the temperature of the earth's atmosphere is gradually increasing.

Impurities: Contaminants or unwanted substances.

Slurry: A mixture of water, wood pulp, and de-inking chemicals.

4

The Endless Voyage of a Glittery Glass Bottle

If you were a glass bottle, you could live forever. That's because glass can be recycled over and over again as many times as you like.

The recycling process for this useful packaging material is very simple. Old bottles are broken up into tiny pieces, added to a new batch of raw materials, and melted. About a third of the new glass you'll find in the United States today was something else in a former life.

Come along on a visit to a glass manufacturing plant and find out exactly how that happens.

Getting Your Glass Ready

1. Return deposit bottles to the store. Save the others.

2. Remove metal caps and rings.

3. Rinse well.

4. Sort the glass containers by color—clear, brown, green—if your program requires it.

5. Don't break them!

What's the Good of It?

If you toss a glass bottle or jar into the garbage, it ends up buried in a landfill, stockpiled for eternity. Or it's taken to an incinerator where it's burned up, wasting a lot of energy and all of the materials from which the glass was made.

When you save glass for recycling, however, you are accomplishing several things. First, you're reducing the amount of garbage that your community must get rid of. Glass bottles are bulky so they take up a lot of space in the garbage trucks. And it's very heavy. Your town pays a "tipping fee" for every ton of solid waste it dumps at a landfill or an incinerator. It is expensive to dump a load with a lot of glass in it.

Second, recycling cuts down on the amounts of raw materials that are needed. Melted down, the materials in the old bottles never lose their special qualities. They are always just as good as new.

Third, and even more important, making new glass out of reclaimed bottles requires much less heat than starting from scratch, so recycling saves energy.

What Will It Become?

Glass bottles and jars are usually recycled into more bottles and jars. As a matter of fact, most new bottles today contain the ghosts of their ancestors.

But some glass is transformed into other handy products. It may be turned into glass "wool" insulation for homes and office buildings. Simply crushed, it can be mixed with other materials to become "glasphalt" for paving streets. It can even become an ingredient in bricks, sewer pipes, reflective paints, and the grit that goes into chicken feed.

And some glass bottles can go back to the store

for recycling. If your state has a "bottle law" that says consumers must pay a deposit on bottles of soft drinks and beer, it makes sense to return them and get your deposit back. Most of them will be sterilized and used again. Another form of recycling!

Rules to Remember

There's very little preparation you need to do when you recycle your glass bottles and jars. First, remove the lids and caps, because these contaminants can damage the melting furnaces and cause defects in the new products. Don't worry about the labels—they will be burned off by the heat.

In many communities, you are asked to separate your glass bottles into their three basic colors: clear (or "flint"), green, and brown. In other places, you may be allowed to send them off all mixed up together. If they are mixed, the colors will be sorted by workers at a MRF before the glass is trucked off to a mill.

It's important that the colors are separated if new glass products are to be made out of the old bottles because, once glass is colored, the color is permanent. It can't be removed like the ink on a newspaper. When brown and green and clear glass bottles are melted together, they turn into a very unpleasant gray-green color that nobody likes.

Anyway, most of the glass made in the United States is clear.

Mixed colors that can't be used for glassmaking, however, are just fine for products like glasphalt and insulation, so some "contaminated" loads of bottles find a home.

Off to the Mill

Container trucks filled to the brim with color-sorted cullet or whole bottles arrive at the glass-making plant and dump their loads in big piles. When it's time to make a new batch of glass, the unbroken bottles are shoved onto wide conveyor belts by workers in bulldozers. The conveyor belts transport them to a machine called a cullet processor.

This great big grinder crushes the bottles into cullet. Of course, if the glass has already been crushed at a MRF, this step is skipped. The cullet is then cleaned with magnets and vacuums, removing contaminants such as metal, pieces of plastic, stones, and dirt.

Now another conveyor takes the cullet to the batch house. Here it is combined in big vats with carefully measured amounts of new raw materials—sand, soda ash, and limestone—and fed into red-hot furnaces where the temperature may go as high as 2,800 degrees Fahrenheit.

Melted by the high temperature, the mixture becomes molten glass that bubbles and churns like a big sea of boiling red soup.

Now it's all ready to become new glass products. For bottles or jars, the molten glass is dropped in measured blobs (known as "gobs") into individual molds. Blasts of compressed air force it against the bottom and sides of the molds and, in only a few seconds, you've got brand-new bottles.

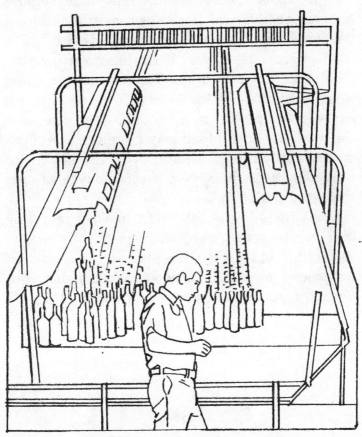

Heated again and cooled slowly, the bottles are closely inspected and packed for shipping. Next time you see them, they'll be decked out in labels and lined up in the grocery store full of mayonnaise, applesauce, pickle relish, or your favorite kind of soda.

What You Can't Recycle

Some kinds of glass are different from the pure glass in bottles and jars. They melt at different temperatures and contain materials that can't be used by most recyclers. Throwing them into the glass bins at your drop-off center or including them with the bottles for curbside pickup can cause lots of problems. If enough of them get into the load, the entire load may be rejected because of "contamination," sending it to the landfill or the incinerator. So be very careful to deposit only the right kinds of glass.

Don't include the following in your recycling bin, unless your community specifically allows them: light bulbs, drinking glasses, heat-resistant ovenware, mirrors, windows, windshields, fish tanks, crystal, china, pottery, or ceramics.

Glossary

Eternity: Forever.

Insulation: Material that prevents the leakage of heat, sound, electricity, etc.

Molten: Melted into liquid form.

Solid waste: Garbage and trash.

Tipping fee: Dumping fee; the money a community must pay for dumping garbage at a landfill or incinerator.

Transformed: Changed.

How to Be an
Environmentally Smart Shopper

What to Do:

- Choose products wrapped in packaging that is recyclable in your community.

- Buy recycled products in recycled containers when possible.

- Buy things in the simplest possible packaging. Ninety percent of wrappings goes right into the garbage can.

- Buy products in returnable, refillable, or reusable containers.

- Save your grocery bags and take them with you to use again on your next shopping trip. Or save them and deposit them in the store's recycling bins. Or take your own cloth or string bags.

- For one or two small items, tell the clerk, "No bag, thank you." But save your receipt to prove that you bought the merchandise.

40

- Buy in large quantities when possible. You get more product and less package. And you may save money.

- Buy things that will last a long time.

- Think twice before buying anything. Are you choosing it out of habit or convenience when something else would be better for the environment?

———————

What Not to Do:

- Don't buy anything unless you really need it.

- Avoid "disposables," things that are good only once or twice and are designed to be thrown right away.

- Avoid single-serving packaging, over-packaging, and individually wrapped items such as cereal boxes, cheese slices, and juices.

- Don't buy paper plates or cups except for special occasions like picnics. Don't throw plastic plates, cups, or eating utensils away. Wash them and use them over and over again.

5

Once Is Not Enough—
The Many Lives of
Plastics

Have you given any serious thought to your shampoo bottle? Has it ever occurred to you that, in a former life, it may have spent some time as a jar of peanut butter, a detergent container, or a soda bottle? And that, when you're through with it, it could very well come back again as your bedroom carpet, a bathtub, a sleeping bag, a scouring pad, a new bottle, or the insides of a shoulder pad?

Plastics, long the pet peeve of the people who are trying to keep the planet from being overwhelmed by garbage, can have many lives. That's because they, too, have proved to be recyclable. At least some varieties of them have, and scientists are busily searching for economical ways to go around again with the others.

Getting Your Plastics Ready

1. Return deposit bottles to the store. Save the others.

2. Remove caps and closures, if required.

3. Rinse well.

4. Include only the types of plastic your town wants.

5. Squash them, if you like.

It's a Mystery!

The problem with plastics is that they are so mysterious. They may look alike but they are a mixed bag of materials, made mostly from fossil fuels such as crude oil and natural gas. What they all have in common is that they are polymers, which means they consist of super molecules, made by stringing together thousands of smaller molecules called monomers.

There are hundreds of types of plastics today, and each one of them is made with its own recipe, using different chemical ingredients or the same ones arranged in another way. To be most valuable for recycling, the plastics must be carefully segregated by type before they can be turned into new products.

Handy But Hard to Hide

Because they are so useful, versatile, and convenient, plastics have become the portion of our garbage that's growing the fastest. Just consider that Americans go through about four million plastic bottles an hour! And that everything we buy today seems to be wrapped in layers of packaging that goes straight from the store into the garbage can.

So what's the matter with that? A lot. Plastics don't weigh much but they take up much space in a garbage truck or a landfill. Once they are buried in a landfill, they may be out of sight but they'll never go away because bacteria and fungi aren't interested in attacking them. Burning them in incinerators gets rid of them—in fact, plastics generate more electrical power per pound than coal when burned—but it wastes valuable raw materials.

Going Around Again

One way to prolong the usefulness of the plastics in our lives is to think of other things to do with them. For example, pack your lunch in empty containers made of plastic that you can't recycle. Keep them handy for storing leftovers in the refrigerator. Line the garbage pail with supermarket bags. Grow seedlings for your garden in used food trays. Make a bird feeder out of a bottle.

Other ways you can help: Try not to buy things wrapped in unnecessary packaging. Buy products that last longer or can be used indefinitely. Avoid "disposables" such as plastic plates, cups, and forks—unless you wash them and use them over and over again or they are included in your recycling program. Ask your parents to choose groceries that are packed in containers that are recyclable where you live. Buy products made of recycled materials.

Saving the Right Kinds of Plastics

Today most types of plastics can be recycled. But no material is truly recyclable unless there's a market for it. That means there's somebody who is willing to buy it and make it into something new. Right now, there are good markets for just two kinds of plastics. One is PET (polyethylene terephthalate), the kind used in soda bottles. The other is HDPE (high-density polyethylene), often used for milk jugs and detergent bottles. That's why most recycling programs want you to save only PET and HDPE and nothing else.

Check out the number codes imprinted on the bottoms of most plastic containers. The codes identify the types of plastics they are made of. Find out which ones are acceptable for recycling in your community and be very careful not to include any of the others. The eager beaver who adds the wrong kinds of materials to the plastics bin may ruin a whole load. And even if the load isn't ruined, somebody's going to have to remove those contaminants before it's fit for a new start in life.

To find out if a plastic container is made out of PET or HDPE, turn it over and look at the triangular symbol on the bottom. If the number 1 is imprinted in the triangle, it is PET. If the number 2 is imprinted, it is HDPE. The symbols look like this:

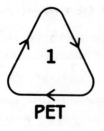

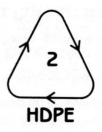

It won't be long before most other kinds of plastics will be easily recyclable too. But for now, wait until your program finds buyers for them and asks you to save them.

Your Job? A Piece of Cake!

If your state has a bottle law requiring you to pay a deposit on soft-drink bottles when you buy them, take these bottles back to the store and get your money back. If you don't want to be bothered doing that, you may include them with your recyclables.

Preparing your plastics for recycling is a piece of cake. First, remove the bottle caps. Second, rinse out the containers. Don't worry about the labels. Third, squash them, if you can, so they'll take up less space. And finally, take them to the recycling center or, if your recyclables are collected at the curb, put them out on your special pickup day.

Okay, your job's done, but their trip has just begun. Want to follow a truckload of plastics on their way to a new life and see what happens to them? Let's go!

Off to Market

When a truckload of mixed recyclables leaves your town, it probably goes to a MRF or a plastics

47

handler where the plastics are separated by type and sometimes by color. Workers sort them one by one as they move along conveyors before being dumped into balers.

The baling machines mash them, squeeze them tight, and tie them up in big cubes or bales that weigh about 800 pounds apiece. Packing loose materials in bales makes them easier to handle and cheaper to transport.

What Happens at the Processing Plant

Shipped off now to a plastics processing plant, the bales of plastics are dumped out of the truck and untied. Then the bottles are jumbled up by a machine called a bale breaker.

The next step is to push them into a granulator, a big grinder that chips them up into little flakes that look like pieces of hard confetti. Sometimes the chips are then air-classified, which means that currents of air blast off most of the dust, paper labels, and other lightweight materials from the heavier chips.

Now the flakes are poured into a giant blender and swirled around with hot water and detergent to remove any remaining contaminants such as labels, glue, food, and dirt.

Some processing plants accept mixed bottles and, in that case, the unsorted plastic chips are pumped into a hydrocyclone or a flotation tank

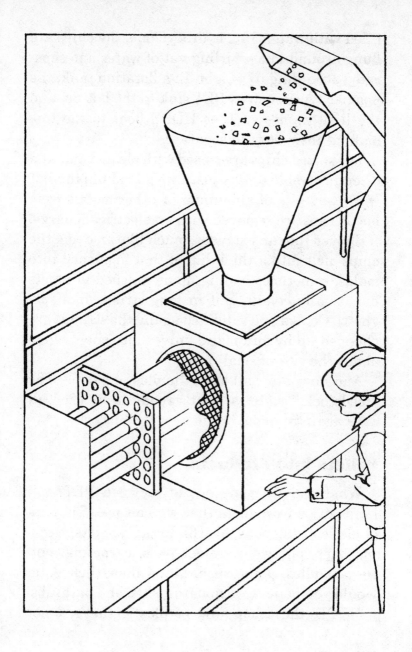

filled with water. In a hydrocyclone, the chips are flung around in a whirling vat of water and separated according to weight. In a flotation tank, the heavier types such as PET sink to the bottom and the lighter ones such as HDPE float to the top, making them easy to separate.

The sorted chips are rinsed with clean water and dried in tumble dryers just like a load of laundry, while any bits of aluminum or other metals from bottle caps are removed with an electrical charge.

Shoved into an extruder, much like an oven, the chips melt into a thick liquid that is pushed into molds, sometimes ending up as finished products but usually coming out in long strings like spaghetti. Cooled and solidified again, the strands are chopped up by automatic knives into tiny pellets about the size of small peas.

And now, after all that, the plastic has become "feedstock," material that's ready to be used all over again to make brand-new products.

Pellets into Products

What can be made out of recycled PET? All kinds of end products that we can use. They include scouring pads, fiberfill for ski jackets, sleeping bags, pillows, shoulder pads, carpeting, bottles, handles, paintbrushes, and floor tiles. And, would you believe, surfboards, skis, and bathtubs!

HDPE, the other kind of plastic that's a hot

ticket today, can be made into such things as trash cans, more bottles, crates, flowerpots, garden furniture, traffic cones, road barriers, pails, fence posts, pipes, and pigpens!

Even a Use for Mixed-Up Plastics

Even unsorted plastics, different types and colors all mixed up together, have their uses. They can become plastic "lumber" for boat docks and piers, fencing, park benches, and playground equipment. This lumber can be sawed, planed, drilled, nailed, and screwed just like real wood but, unlike wood, it is resistant to chemicals and insects and so it is very practical to use outdoors.

Glossary

Economical: Inexpensive; practical.

End products: Final products; results.

Fossil fuels: Fuels—coal, petroleum, and natural gas—that were formed millions of years ago and must be dug out of the earth.

Segregated: Set apart.

Solidified: Became solid.

Versatile: Flexible; handy.

6

Can a Steel Can Can It Again?

You've eaten your chicken noodle soup and gulped your fruit juice. Puffy has consumed the contents of a can of salmon delight and Fido has finished his beef bits. You are left with the empty cans. Stop! Don't throw them in the garbage pail! Save them for recycling. Those cans are now scrap metal, a valuable material that's eagerly sought by hungry steel mills.

"Tin" cans are made out of steel (made from iron ore and steel scrap) with a thin protective coating of tin on the surface. They are a snap to recycle. They are simply melted and used all over again. And again. And again. They can be recycled forever without losing any of their important properties. In fact, steel is America's most recycled material.

Any used steel product may become the raw material for any other steel product. So the recycled cans from your house may become part of a bridge or a shiny new station wagon. They may be transformed into new cans of chicken noodle soup, salmon delight, or beef bits. Or a lot of other things like frying pans, washing machines, bicycles, paper clips, mattress springs, structural steel beams, railroad cars, and chain-link fences.

Getting Your Steel Cans Ready

1. Return deposit cans to the store. Save the others.

2. Rinse them out.

3. Include tops and bottoms.

Save Your Cans

Save your cans and anything else that's made out of metal, such as wire hangers, old tools, toys, nails, rusty pails, broken garden furniture, bike frames, food trays, foil, bottle caps, and lids. Toss them in your town's small-metals recycling bins, or include them in your curbside pickups. Don't forget to include the ends of the cans. They are valuable too. So are empty, dry paint cans and aerosol cans. The big metal things like refrigerators and hot-water boilers are probably collected separately in your town but they will end up in the same place as the cans.

All you have to do to get a can ready for recycling is to give it a good rinse. Don't bother to remove the paper labels. Include any cans, even "bimetals," the kind with steel bodies and aluminum ends.

Doing Your Bit for the Environment

Americans go through about 100 million steel cans a day—and every one of them is recyclable. One good reason for saving them for recycling is to get them out of the waste stream, the garbage that's headed for the incinerator or the landfill. Steel doesn't burn up in an incinerator. It does degrade into iron oxide when it is exposed to air and moisture in a landfill, but it takes a lot of years to do it.

All new steel products today are made at least partially out of recycled steel. Some contain nothing but scrap, including automobiles chopped up into little pieces, cut-up railroad cars, industrial machinery, even the steel hulls of ocean-going freighters, and, of course, steel cans.

When you recycle steel, you're helping to preserve natural resources and the land that would have been mined for new raw materials. Every time a ton of steel cans is recycled, it saves 2,500 pounds of iron ore, 1,000 pounds of coal, and 40 pounds of limestone.

It reduces air and water pollution, and it saves energy too. Enough energy is saved each year to power more than 18 million households.

Hit the Road with a Steel Can

On its way to becoming something else, a steel can travels along a rugged route. The first stop is at a MRF or a scrap yard.

If, in your community, the cans are collected all mixed up together with other recyclables, they will go probably straightaway to a MRF. Dumped on the floor or into a receiving pit, they are loaded onto a conveyor with the rest of the things. Steel is ferrous (made with iron), so, as everything moves along the conveyor, it's easy to pick it out with big magnets and dump it down its own chute into a bin. Compacted and baled into heavy cubes called "bundles," it's soon ready for the next part of its journey.

But, if your town asks you to segregate your metals from the other recyclables, then they are more likely to be carted away to a scrap yard instead of a MRF. The scrap processor separates all the steel from the other metals, grades them, and cleans them. The processor then sells the steel directly to a mill or a metals broker who finds a mill that wants it.

Detinning: Short Stop Along the Way

Sometimes the cans are recycled just the way they are, tin and all. But often they make a detour, going first to a detinner to have the thin protective coating of tin removed.

At most detinners, the cans start off in a big grinder that shreds them into skinny pieces. Then blasts of air pull out the labels and dirt, and powerful magnets separate the steel from any other metals that may have found their way into the load. Now, the shredded cans are shoved into a big basket. The basket is lowered into a tub filled with an electrically charged chemical solution.

This "electrolytic bath" dissolves the tin, leaving only the steel in solid form. But the tin is valuable, so it is recycled too. The chemical solution is pumped into a tank where the dissolved tin

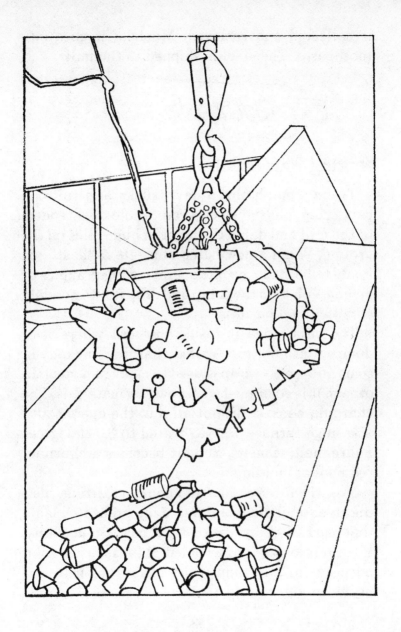

is collected and removed. Much of it goes into toothpaste! The steel is shipped to the mill.

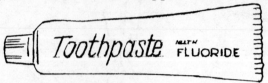

Making New Steel

Twenty-four hours a day, trucks and railroad cars bring loads of steel scrap, whole or shredded, to the mill and dump them out in huge piles on the ground. When a new batch of steel—a "heat"—is ready to be made, people operating big grapples or magnets pick up the scrap and drop it into gondola cars that run on rails.

The cars move it inside the mill where it is dumped into big tubs called charging buckets. In some mills, only scrap is used to make new steel. In others, it is combined with new raw materials. The charging buckets drop it all into the open mouth of a huge furnace where, heated to 3,000 degrees Fahrenheit, it melts. Soon it becomes a churning red pool of molten steel.

Now the furnace tilts and pours a spitting, hissing river of liquid metal into a big preheated ladle that carries it by crane to a casting machine. Poured into molds and cooled, it turns into a solid once again, all ready to be made into new and useful products.

Glossary

Crane: A machine with a movable arm for lifting heavy weights.

Detinner: A company that removes the tin from steel cans.

Ferrous: Containing iron.

Gondola car: An open-topped container car that runs on rails.

Grapple: A device with strong movable prongs that grasp and pick up heavy things.

Iron ore: Natural material in the ground that contains iron.

Iron oxide: Rust; a chemical combination of iron and oxygen.

Scrap: Materials that have completed their useful life or pieces left over from manufacturing.

Let's Talk Batteries

All batteries, large or small, are hazardous to the environment. They contain dangerously toxic chemicals such as mercury, cadmium, lead, and sulfuric acid. Thrown in the garbage and buried, their casings eventually crack, allowing the chemicals to leak into the soil and the ground water. Incinerated, the harmful substances escape into the air as gas or are left in the ashes that are sent off to be buried.

In many states, service stations are required to accept old car and motorcycle batteries *and* recycle them. And many community drop-off centers now take batteries of all kinds for recycling. Sometimes retail stores that sell them will take them back for safe disposal. If none of these opportunities is available to your family, save your dead batteries—car and motorcycle as well as all kinds of household batteries including button types—and include them with your toxic wastes (see page 61).

Caution! It's Toxic!

Don't throw toxic chemicals into the garbage. Don't pour them down the drain or in the sewer. Don't dump them on the ground. Don't bury them. Don't throw them in the lake, the river, or the ocean. Take them to a hazardous waste center or give them to someone who needs them.

What are toxic wastes? Pesticides, paints, paint removers and thinners, acids, alcohols, gasoline, disinfectants, bleach, oven and toilet-bowl cleaners, drain cleaners, degreasers, photographic chemicals, swimming-pool chemicals, solvents, weed killers, art supplies, furniture polish, antifreeze, batteries, adhesives, motor oil, tires, and more. If you aren't certain of a chemical's environmental safety, consider it toxic and treat it accordingly.

For the nearest hazardous waste center and the times you may use it, call your local officials or your county's Department of Health. Ask if there is a periodic hazardous-waste collection day in your community. If not, suggest that one should be started.

Index

A

aluminum, 5
aquifers, 5

B

batteries, 60
biodegrade, 5
bottles, 14, 32–38

C

cullet, 14

D

detinner, 56

E

end user, 13
environment, 23–24, 60

F

food scraps, 9
fossil fuels, 43

G

garbage, 3–8
glass, 2, 32–38
global warming, 23

H

hazardous waste
  center, 61
HDPE (high-density
  polyethylene), 46,
  50–51

I

incinerators, 5–6
insulation, 34
iron ore, 53
iron oxide, 54

M

MRF (materials
  recovery facility), 2,
  12–14, 16, 55–56
metal, 12, 14, 54

N

newspapers, 1, 3, 6,
  12–13, 23–31

P

paper, 5
PET (polyethylene
  terephthalate),
  45–46, 50
photodegrade, 5
plastics, 3, 5, 11–12,
  14–15, 42–51
pollution, 6, 24, 55
polymers, 43
pulper, 27–29

L

landfills, 3–6, 34

R

raw materials, 2
recyclables, 2–3

T

tin cans, 1, 56–58
toxic residues, 5–6, 61
toxic waste, 61
transfer station, 12
trees, 23–24

S

slurry, 27
steel, 52–58

W

waste: *see* garbage
waste stream, 3

CAMELOT WORLD
A FRESH LOOK
AT OUR WORLD